CARTOON★NATION
EST. 1776

DEMOCRACY

by Liam O'Donnell
illustrated by Patricia Storms

CONSULTANT:
Michael Bailey
Colonel William J. Walsh Associate Professor
of American Government
Georgetown University, Washington, D.C.

Capstone
press
Mankato, Minnesota

Graphic Library is published by Capstone Press,
151 Good Counsel Drive, P.O. Box 669, Mankato, Minnesota 56002.
www.capstonepress.com

1 2 3 4 5 6 13 12 11 10 09 08

Library of Congress Cataloging-in-Publication Data
O'Donnell, Liam, 1970–
    Democracy / by Liam O'Donnell; illustrated by Patricia Storms.
    p. cm. — (Graphic library. Cartoon nation)
    Includes bibliographical references and index.
    ISBN-13: 978-1-4296-1332-3 (hardcover)
    ISBN-10: 1-4296-1332-7 (hardcover)
    ISBN-13: 978-1-4296-1781-9 (softcover pbk.)
    ISBN-10: 1-4296-1781-0 (softcover pbk.)
    1. Democracy — Juvenile literature. 2. Democracy — History — Juvenile literature.
3. Democracy — United States — Juvenile literature. I. Storms, Patricia. II. Title. III. Series.
JC423.O257 2008
321.8 — dc22   2007027335

Summary: In political cartoon format, explains the origins of democracy, its spread
    throughout the world, and its role in United States government and society.

Art Director and Designer
Bob Lentz

Cover Artist
Kelly Brown

Editor
Christopher L. Harbo

TABLE OF CONTENTS

★ Pizza and Politics 4

★ The First Democracy 6

★ More Romans and Monarchs 8

★ Books to the Rescue..................... 10

★ Revolution in America................. 12

★ Birth of a Democracy, Almost 14

★ Democracy Spreads 16

★ Changing the U.S. Constitution..... 18

★ Delicious Democracy Ingredients ... 20

★ Voting: Pots and People 22

★ Democracy Distractions............... 24

★ Nurturing Democracy 26

Time Line 28
Glossary 30
Read More 31
Internet Sites 31
Index 32

PIZZA AND POLITICS

Has your family ever disagreed on what to order for dinner? What did you do? Maybe you took a vote to choose.

There's three of them and one of you, so no pizza tonight. It might not sound fair, but it is because most of the family wanted chicken. The next time you order food, your sister and mom might vote for pizza and you will get what you want.

Many governments are run the same way. From pizza to politics, when we debate issues and do what the largest number of people wants to do, we're taking part in democracy.

Democracy started in ancient Greece. In this type of political system, people have an equal right to have their opinions count in government. The people also choose their leaders and give them the power to make decisions.

Did the Greeks have this much trouble building their skate parks?

Probably not, but no one ever said democracy was easy.

PEOPLE POWER

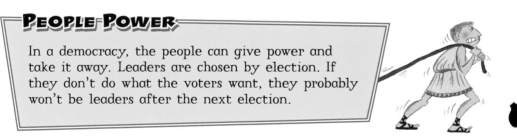

In a democracy, the people can give power and take it away. Leaders are chosen by election. If they don't do what the voters want, they probably won't be leaders after the next election.

More than 2,000 years ago, most countries were **monarchies**. Kings and emperors had all the power. Only a king's family members could be leaders of the country. Things weren't very fair for people born outside the royal family. Most people had no rights and lived in poverty.

Around 508 BC, the Greeks created the world's first democracy in the city of Athens. They divided citizens into four classes, or groups, based on how wealthy they were.

monarchy — a system of government in which the ruler is a king or queen

Citizens from all four classes could attend political meetings and have a say in how their country was run. Democracy in Greece was a success, but it didn't last long.

In 404 BC, a group of rival Greeks called the Spartans took control of Athens. They took away the rights of the Athenian citizens.

A few years later, the Romans defeated the Spartans. The Romans didn't like democracy either. It looked like democracy was gone for good.

LEFT OUT OF DEMOCRACY

Not everybody had a say in Greek democracy. Women and slaves were not considered citizens. They weren't allowed to attend political meetings.

Rome was a republic. Only a few citizens were allowed to make decisions about the country. But that didn't stop them from borrowing some ideas from democracy.

Hello neighbor. Could I borrow some democracy?

For instance, the Romans believed in natural law. They believed that people should be nice and not go around robbing and killing each other. But Roman leaders weren't fair to everyone. They thought they were favored by the gods and they ruled over the peasants and slaves across the Roman lands.

Democracy is a terrible idea.

Can you imagine peasants and slaves running the government?

From back here, democracy sounds like a great idea.

Around AD 476, Roman rule ended and the Middle Ages began. For a thousand years, Europe was divided into monarchies called kingdoms. A few wealthy nobles and kings owned all the land. They ruled over peasants who had no money and no rights.

To stay in power, a king needed the support of rich nobles living throughout the kingdom. Every so often, the king called nobles to a council. He listened to their advice on how to run the kingdom.

This practice was the start of officials representing regions in governments. It's still used in democracies today.

THE MAGNA CARTA

In 1215, angry English nobles forced their ruler, King John, to sign the Magna Carta. This document limited the power of the king and paved the way for modern democracy. For the first time, the king needed permission before making new laws that affected the whole kingdom.

BOOKS TO THE RESCUE

In the 1400s, most Europeans were still very poor and uneducated. Only wealthy people learned to read and write because books were handwritten and very expensive. Without an education, many poor people had no chance to learn that there were other ways to run a country.

Around 1440, Johannes Gutenberg, a German inventor, created a machine that could print many pages of text in a short time. It made books much easier to create and cheaper to buy. Soon, more books were available and more people learned to read.

For the next 300 years, people read books with new ideas for running governments. In many books, authors said that the people should be in charge and not just one greedy king. As more people read about how unfair their governments were, they got angry and decided it was time for a change.

WHAT PEOPLE WERE READING

What was getting people so worked up? Well, some writers had pretty revolutionary ideas about running a government . . .

| John Locke *Second Treatise of Civil Government* 1690 | Charles de Montesquieu *The Spirit of Laws* 1748 | Jean-Jacques Rousseau *The Social Contract* 1762 |

In the 1700s, Britain ruled the American colonies. The British government forced the colonists to pay taxes on newspapers, playing cards, and even tea. The colonists became angry about paying taxes because they had no representation in British government.

Britain also passed a group of laws the colonists called the Intolerable Acts. One act forced the colonists to feed British soldiers and give them a place to sleep at night.

By 1776, Thomas Jefferson, an American leader, was busy writing down his ideas for running a country in the Declaration of Independence. He wrote that all men are equal and they have rights that the government can't take away. In the 1700s, these were new ideas.

When the colonists won the Revolutionary War in 1783, they didn't want another monarchy. They wanted citizens to have a say in how the new country was run. They wanted democracy.

In 1787, the leaders of America wrote the U.S. **Constitution**. It listed the rules for running the government and made sure fair laws were created. A new kind of democracy was born.

constitution — the system of laws that state the rights of the people and the powers of the government

American citizens now had power in Congress, where the laws for the United States are made. But America wasn't a true democracy yet. The **Founding Fathers** were wealthy men. Some were afraid of being robbed if the common people controlled the government.

The revolution is over. The people are in charge. Isn't that great?

Yes, it's terrific. Now, if you'll excuse me, I'm going home to hide my money!

Founding Father — one of a handful of men who were important in helping the colonies become one country

Most of the Founding Fathers thought that the United States was too big to be run as a democracy. A few even called the people "the great beast." They said that running the government would be too chaotic if every person was allowed to take part.

THE GREAT BEAST

The Founding Fathers did give the people some powers. In each state, people elected leaders to speak for them and make laws in the House of Representatives in Congress. Citizens finally had representation in government — something they never had under British rule.

The people now had a voice in government. The United States was on its way to becoming the world's first democracy in nearly 2,000 years.

But not everybody was equal during early American democracy. Just like in ancient Greece, women were not allowed to vote. Even after the American Revolution most African Americans were slaves and not allowed to vote.

News about the American Revolution traveled around the world. Soon, people in other countries wanted change too. In the late 1700s, people in France were starving and their king had spent all the country's money.

Those Americans had the right idea. Maybe we should start a French Revolution.

Ah, Pierre, I think you're on to something!

By 1792, the people of France had kicked their king off the throne and out of power. After the revolution, France was controlled by a small group of people. Then in 1799, a general named Napoleon Bonaparte took control of the country. France was free of a monarchy, but it wasn't a democracy.

NAPOLEON AS A BOY

NAPOLEON AS A MAN

Emperor Napoleon won't share power with anyone!

I was hoping he'd outgrow that!

In 1848, well after Napoleon's rule, France finally started down the road to democracy. The new government, called the Second Republic, included a representative parliament where elected officials could make laws.

Being free to say what you think is a key part of democracy. But after the French Revolution, people in France had to be very careful about what they said. People who supported the king or spoke out against the revolution were jailed or killed. No wonder that period in history is called the "Reign of Terror."

Just a little off the top. And don't forget to trim my mustache!

I'm an executioner, not a barber!

Aside from a nasty civil war in the 1600s, England's road to democracy was peaceful and slow. Very slow. It started in 1215 when British nobles forced King John to sign the Magna Carta. Over the next 600 years, the people demanded more rights and representation in government.

ROAD TO DEMOCRACY ONLY 492 MORE YEARS TO GO!

Are we there yet?

Not even close.

Today, Great Britain has a constitutional monarchy. Citizens elect representatives to a democratic parliament and the monarchy has very little power.

No democracy is perfect. During the early years of the United States, democracy wasn't even close to being perfect. Congress favored the wealthy, and women and slaves couldn't vote.

The American people improved their democracy by making **amendments** to the U.S. Constitution. A good constitution must have strong laws and it must leave room for new laws to be added or changed.

The most common way to amend the U.S. Constitution is to have both the House of Representatives and the Senate agree to the amendment. Then, every state votes on the amendment. Three-fourths of the states must agree to the amendment before it is added to the Constitution.

Have a nice trip!

Send us a postcard!

amendment — a change made to a law or a legal document

The U.S. Constitution has been amended 27 times. The first 10 amendments were made in 1791. Together they are known as the Bill of Rights. The 27th Amendment, limiting pay raises for members of Congress, was first suggested in 1789. It wasn't made official until 1992!

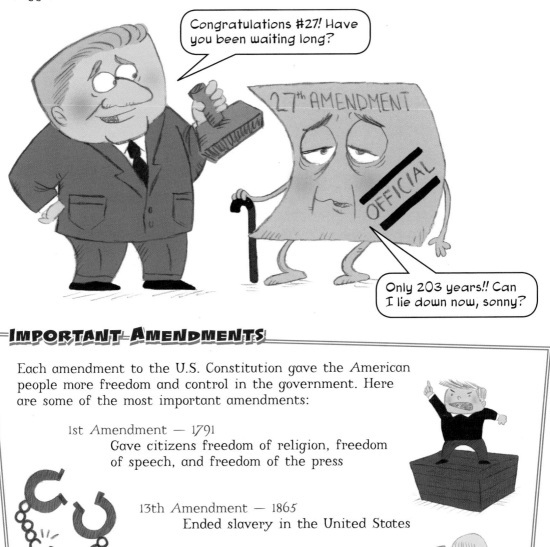

Congratulations #27! Have you been waiting long?

27th AMENDMENT

OFFICIAL

Only 203 years!! Can I lie down now, sonny?

IMPORTANT AMENDMENTS

Each amendment to the U.S. Constitution gave the American people more freedom and control in the government. Here are some of the most important amendments:

1st Amendment — 1791
Gave citizens freedom of religion, freedom of speech, and freedom of the press

13th Amendment — 1865
Ended slavery in the United States

19th Amendment — 1920
Allowed women to vote in elections

VOTING BOOTH

22nd Amendment — 1951
Limited presidents to two terms in office

Ahhh, shucks!

DELICIOUS DEMOCRACY INGREDIENTS

Making a democracy is a little like baking a cake. Mix the ingredients into a sticky batter, and — okay, maybe it's not that much like baking a cake. But democracy does need the right ingredients.

Mom! Where's the jar of Freedom of Speech?

Your dad used it up making his Chili Freedom Fries.

Down with the evil vegetables!

Freedom is important to democracy. Freedom of speech allows people to say what they think. Freedom of the press allows the media to criticize the government. Freedom of assembly allows people to gather together to discuss the way their country is run.

In a democracy, citizens can get involved in government. Almost anyone can be elected, no matter how little money they have or who they know.

REGISTRATION OFFICE

APPLICATION

Sorry, kid. Come back in about 30 years.

YOU MUST BE AT LEAST 35 YEARS OLD TO BE PRESIDENT OF THE UNITED STATES

Democracies must also have fair laws that apply to everyone, including the leaders of the country and the military. This rule of law protects citizens against leaders abusing their powers in government.

That was strike three!

But as president, I should get four strikes!

Mr. President, you can't change the rules just because your team is losing.

OTHER JOBS

Many famous democratic leaders were not always politicians. These are just a few of the leaders who had cool jobs before leading a democracy:

Ronald Reagan was a Hollywood actor before becoming U.S. president.

Mary McAleese was a journalist before serving as president of Ireland.

Tommy Douglas was a Baptist minister before he became premier of Saskatchewan in Canada.

VOTING: POTS AND PEOPLE

People power is what makes democracy work. Every few years, democratic countries have elections to let the people choose who will run the country. In fact, some voting in ancient Greece was done by writing names on broken pottery.

Why is your dad so angry?

He's not mad. He's getting ready to vote.

Why are you hitting our voting machine?

How else am I going to break it into ballots?

Today, people vote by writing on a piece of paper called a ballot or using a computer. In most elections, the **candidate** with the most votes wins the election.

Candidates in elections often belong to a political party. Members of a political party share the same views about how a country should be run. In the United States, the two main political parties are the Democrats and the Republicans. Other countries, like Canada and the United Kingdom, have three or more political parties involved in government.

POLITICAL PARTY MEETING

Hi! I'm ready to join the party.

candidate — a person who runs for elected office

Elections in a democracy must be fair. Elections are fair when voters can choose among several candidates with different views. In the United States, most major offices have several candidates on the ballot.

Too bad people can only vote for one of us.

In a democracy, elections are carefully monitored to prevent cheating. Independent observers watch the voting and ballot counting.

Hi! I'm the independent observer for this election.

This clown can't be serious.

COMPUTER VOTING

Using a computer to vote in an election is called electronic voting, or e-voting. Some people think e-voting is easier and faster than using paper ballots. Others say that the e-voting computers often break down and can be tampered with to show inaccurate voting results.

DEMOCRACY DISTRACTIONS

Even after all those battles for more freedom, some people today don't seem very interested in democracy. In some U.S. elections, less than half the people vote.

Democracy succeeds when people are well educated and know what's going on in their country. Learning about current events, staying in school, and getting involved in your community are great ways to help democracy grow where you live.

Whether you live in a big city or a tiny town, elected officials represent you in the government. Cities and towns in the United States have mayors who are elected to make decisions. Working with the mayor are city council members who are elected to represent specific neighborhoods in your city or town.

Your bosses are here!

CITY COUNCIL CHAMBER

Don't keep them waiting! Send them in.

Hello bosses. What can I do for you?

This council member represents your neighborhood. She is responsible for listening to the people who live there. That means you!

LEVELS OF GOVERNMENT

The U.S. democracy has three levels of government:

National — deals with issues concerning the country and how the United States works with other nations of the world. The national leader is the president.

State — takes care of what happens in your state and how your state works with other states in the country. The state leader is the governor.

Municipal — decides what happens in your city or town. The leader of the municipal government is often the mayor.

Around the world, democracy is growing. In the 1950s, the world had 22 democracies. Today, more than 100 countries are democracies.

Like a plant that needs someone to water it, democracy needs people who are willing to work to make it grow.

In most democracies, you must be 18 years old to vote or run in an election. But there are many ways you can help democracy grow before your 18th birthday. Take the time to listen to the ideas of someone you disagree with.

Because I believe in democracy, I will listen to you tell me why I have to go to bed.

Vote with your friends on what game to play, instead of arguing.

Each of these ideas shows that you believe in democracy. When you're old enough to vote, you'll be choosing the next leader of your city, state, or country. It could be someone in who lives on your street or goes to your school.

Who knows? It could be you!

TIME LINE

508 BC — Democracy is born in Athens, Greece.

508 BC

404 BC — The Spartans conquer Athens and end democracy in Greece.

404 BC

1787 — The U.S. Constitution is written and begins its path toward democracy.

TO DEMOCRACY

U.S. CONSTITUTION

1787

1776 — Thomas Jefferson writes the Declaration of Independence. It says people have rights that the government can't take away.

DECLARATION OF INDEPENDENCE

1776

1789 — The French Revolution begins in France. People rebel against King Louis XVI, demanding more freedom.

1789

1791 — The Bill of Rights, containing 10 amendments, is added to the U.S. Constitution. The United States becomes more democratic.

BILL OF RIGHTS

CONSTITUTION

1791

1215 — English nobles force King John to sign the Magna Carta. From then on the king needed the nobles' permission to make certain laws.

1215

MAGNA CARTA

1440 — Johannes Gutenberg invents movable type, allowing more people to read about democracy.

1440

1775 — The American Revolutionary War begins when American colonists fight with British troops in Lexington, Massachusetts.

BOOM!

1775

1848 — Demands for democratic reforms sweep across Hungary, Austria, Italy, Germany, and other European countries.

DEMOCRACY

1848

2007 — Democracy takes off. More than 100 countries have democratic governments.

DEMOCRACY

2007

GLOSSARY

amendment (uh-MEND-muhnt) — a change made to a law or a legal document

ballot (BAL-uht) — a punch card, piece of paper, or electronic screen on which a person's vote is recorded

candidate (KAN-duh-dayt) — a person who runs for elected office

citizen (SIT-i-zuhn) — a person who is part of a nation by birth or choice

Congress (KONG-griss) — the part of the U.S. government that makes laws for the country; Congress has two parts called the House of Representatives and Senate.

constitution (kon-stuh-TOO-shuhn) — the system of laws that state the rights of the people and the powers of the government

Founding Father (FOUN-ding FAH-thur) — one of a handful of men who were important in helping the colonies become one country

monarchy (MON-urk-ee) — a system of government in which the ruler is a king or queen

parliament (PAR-luh-muhnt) — the group of people who have been elected to make laws in some countries

peasant (PEZ-uhnt) — a person in Europe who owned a small farm or worked on a farm

politics (POL-uh-tiks) — the activities of politicians and political parties

republic (ri-PUHB-lik) — a form of government in which the people have the power to elect representatives who manage the government

READ MORE

Brown, Liz. *Civics.* Social Studies Essential Skills. New York: Weigl, 2008.

Downing, David. *Democracy.* Political & Economic Systems. Chicago: Heinemann, 2008.

Lansford, Tom. *Democracy.* Political Systems of the World. New York: Marshall Cavendish Benchmark, 2007.

Rees, Peter. *Liberty: Blessing or Burden?* Shockwave. New York: Children's Press, 2008.

Woolf, Alex. *Democracy.* Systems of Government. Milwaukee: World Almanac Library, 2006.

INTERNET SITES

FactHound offers a safe, fun way to find Internet sites related to this book. All of the sites on FactHound have been researched by our staff.

Here's how:
1. Visit *www.facthound.com*
2. Choose your grade level.
3. Type in this book ID **1429613327** for age-appropriate sites. You may also browse subjects by clicking on letters, or by clicking on pictures and words.
4. Click on the **Fetch It** button.

FactHound will fetch the best sites for you!

INDEX

amendments, 18–19, 28
American Revolution, 12–13,
    14, 15, 16, 29

ballots, 22, 23
Bill of Rights, 19, 28
Bonaparte, Napoleon, 16
books, 10–11

candidates, 22, 23
citizens, 6, 7, 8, 9, 13, 14,
    15, 17, 19, 21
Congress, 14, 15, 18, 19

Declaration of Independence,
    12, 28

education, 10, 24
elections, 5, 19, 22–23, 24,
    26, 27
Europe, 9, 10, 29

Founding Fathers, 14–15
freedom, 19, 20, 24, 28
French Revolution, 16, 17, 28

Great Britain, 12, 15, 17, 29
Greece, 5, 6–7, 15, 22, 28
Gutenberg, Johannes, 10, 29

Jefferson, Thomas, 12, 28

leaders, 5, 6, 8, 9, 11, 12, 13,
    15, 21, 24, 25, 27
Locke, John, 11

Magna Carta, 9, 17, 29
monarchies, 6, 9, 13, 16, 17
Montesquieu, Charles de, 11

natural law, 8

political parties, 22
printing press, 10

Reign of Terror, 17
rights, 5, 6, 7, 9, 12, 13, 17,
    19, 20, 28
Romans, 7, 8, 9
Rousseau, Jean-Jacques, 11
rule of law, 21

U.S. Constitution, 13,
    18–19, 28

voting, 4, 11, 15, 18, 19, 22, 23,
    24, 26, 27